AF881330

Charged With A DUI In Pennsylvania?

Useful Info Revealed That May Help You In Your Case

Lee A. Ciccarelli, Esq.

Copyright © 2015 by Lee A. Ciccarelli, Esq.

All rights reserved. No part of this book may be used or reproduced in any manner whatsoever without written permission of the author.

ISBN: 978-1-941645-59-8

Design and Published by:

Speakeasy Publications

73-03 Bell Blvd #10

Oakland Gardens, N.Y. 11364

www.SpeakeasyMarketingInc.com

888-225-8594

DISCLAIMER

This publication is intended to be informational only. No legal advice is being given, and no attorney-client relationship is intended to be created by reading this material. If you are facing legal issues, whether criminal or civil, seek professional legal counsel to get your questions answered.

Ciccarelli Law Offices

304 North High Street

West Chester, PA 19380

(610) 692-8700

www.ciccarelli.com

CLIENT TESTIMONIALS

"Lee Cicarelli is both extremely personable and professional. He guided me through a very difficult and intimidating process with his warmth and expertise. I felt confident that he was genuinely concerned with getting the best outcome for me and knew he would work hard to make it happen. I have always been wary of lawyers, but Lee has given me a newfound trust and respect for them. Thank you Lee!!!" **- Grace**

....

"I appreciate everyone's guidance and support at Ciccarelli Law Offices and everyone played a vital role on my behalf. Lee and his office calmed my anxiety and everyone's professionalism was way beyond what I expected. Thank you again. I recommend this firm to everyone. I rate them an A+ firm." **- Gary B.**

....

"Your professionalism and basic concern for my son turned an unhappy event into a valuable and meaningful experience. My hope is to be able to recommend your firm with highest praise. We are thrilled with your expert representation and extraordinary results. Thank you immensely!" **- Janice E.**

TABLE OF CONTENTS

AUTHOR INTRODUCTION

Attorney Lee Ciccarelli has been practicing law for over 25 years, since 1989 and his firm is a litigation firm that has handled thousands of DUI defense cases. He went to Bucknell University as an undergrad. He continued to George Washington University Law School, which is the oldest in the country, where he graduated in 1989. After graduating with a Juris Doctor degree, he returned home where he began his legal career under the tutelage of a presiding judge and learned first-hand about the trial litigation including DUI, Drunk Driving and criminal defense.

Lee's goal was to gain experience from the vantage point of being in court rather than behind a desk in an office, and found his clerkship to be an invaluable experience for him to see a judge presiding over serious criminal and personal injury trials.

He has seen many excellent trial attorneys in criminal cases, specifically DUI cases as well as injury cases. He has observed their process and been able to get input from a very seasoned trial attorney who later became a judge. He later went on to joining one of Pennsylvania's most recognized criminal defense practices.

After years of practice, Lee left central Pennsylvania and relocated to the greater Philadelphia area, specifically in Chester County and started his own litigation practice with a team of lawyers that share his belief and work ethic.

In the 15-16 years since he formed Ciccarelli Law Offices, Lee has become lead counsel for a team of eight other attorneys who are all passionate about their clients and experienced in fighting for them when they need it most.

INTEREST IN DUI DEFENSE

It may sound a little idealistic, but one thing that is so confounding about DUI law is that we live in a society that so heavily emphasizes and financially profits from the sale of alcohol. We are constantly being marketed and prodded to buy and drink alcohol, not just in our homes, but at bars and establishments to which we have to travel. In the same society in which the government and private big interests make money off alcohol, we arrest convict and jail people for being intoxicated, even in situations where there is no accident or serious injury. It seems that the ever increasing penalties are as much a product of politicians looking to bolster their image as public safety.

Over the past 20 years, we have seen lawyers who tend to be politicians and want to move up in the ranks by further criminalizing drunk driving and alcoholism rather than focusing on alcohol as a disease. At the same time people are profiting from alcohol, it's also being criminalized. The dichotomy of that development is a factor that spurs our team to fight for individuals accused of drunk driving and facing severe incarceration and penalties.

Someone who makes a mistake should not be judged too harshly. The reality is, when people get a DUI, that's like a snapshot, probably the worst time of their life and the biggest mistake they have ever made; they shouldn't be judged forever by that. Even for cases in which facts are incontestable and they were operating a motor vehicle while they were inebriated, they have a right to fight to make sure the punishment is fair and calibrated and not overly harsh.

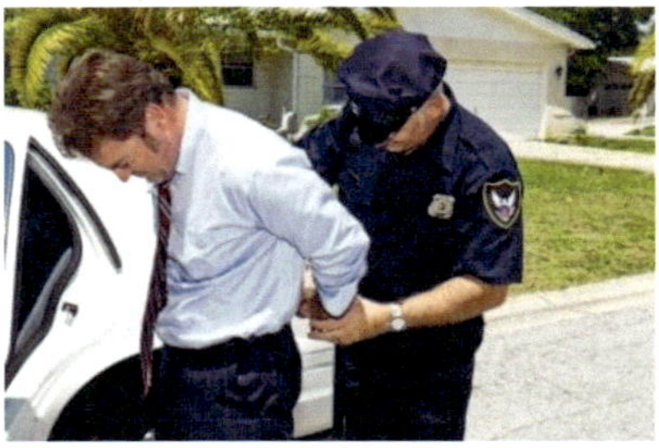

I have a chip on my shoulder when it comes to DUIs and when it comes to politicians and prosecutors; they tend to be the same people, looking to make a name for themselves by overly punishing American citizens. In the past year there were more than 50,000 DUI arrests in Pennsylvania but a study came out in June, called the Wallet hub study, saying that Pennsylvania was one of the least punitive states in the union. In fact we are basically the 49th most lenient state, despite the fact that in Pennsylvania, even a first offense DUI carries mandatory minimum jail time and a 12-month loss of license.

Locations Covered In Pennsylvania

The advantage of having eight or nine attorneys, including attorneys who were former DUI prosecutors, is that even though our main office is in suburban Philadelphia (Chester County Pennsylvania with a population over 500,000) we serve a ten (10) county area comprising the greater Philadelphia metro area, and including Lancaster, Reading & Allentown. We have attorneys who are extremely experienced in the Philadelphia court system, including Delaware county, where we have a former prosecutor; Chester County, where I've been for over 15 years; and Bucks County, between Philadelphia and New Jersey.

Through proper organization and the effots of our team, we have the ability to extend our practice area over a large area; we actually have about 6-7 satellite offices. Rather than having an association with someone who just happens to be there, clients get a very centralized defense practice. The attorneys are based in West Chester, but we travel out to offices in the county where the case is being conducted, but it is essentially managed and advocated by a team.

Top 5 Things To Do After a DUI Arrest

Many friends, and their friends, looking for advice from a seasoned DUI defense attorney reach out to me. Here is what I tell them:

1. They are not a criminal, but a DUI is a serious crime and they cannot treat it like a traffic ticket or ignore it.
2. The time to contact an attorney is immediately after you have been stopped or arrested for a DUI.
3. An experienced DUI attorney does not need to wait for the criminal complaint or paperwork to be able to assess your risks, outline a strategy, and provide you options.
4. The decision to hire an attorney is not easy but you can consider the following:
    a. Is the attorney part of a team or a solo?
    b. Is the attorney experienced in DUI cases?
    c. Is the attorney responsive?
    d. Is the attorney compassionate and concerned?
5. You want an attorney that has the resources to defend you rather than just plea your case and a team can provide that. You want a team that has the experience of handling hundreds and thousands of DUI cases. You want a team of attorneys that cares about your welfare and who has your back.

My team and I have handled thousands of DUIs. We represent regular people who are facing punishments that they often view as surreal. Neither my team nor my clients see themselves as criminals

though they are facing very serious repercussions. I've put together a team of attorneys who have also been prosecutors; some people may wonder why we would hire a prosecutor, but having different perspectives on the team provides insight that we can use to benefit our clients.

Different Perspectives In DUI Defense

Back in 2000, when I started on my own, I was a sole practitioner; for DUI and law like criminal law, it's very common for the lawyer to be a solo practitioner. Fortunately, I developed a good reputation and became so busy that I was running from one court to another to another and I had to make a strategic decision to add an attorney. I also decided 15 years ago to be a vanguard in the use of technology, to not just have other attorneys in my office, but to create a coordinated team, seamlessly working together on cases concurrently, using technology to stay up to speed. For example, attorneys can easily message or Skype each other if an issue comes up, even when they're in court, which gives us the advantage of not just one attorney versus the government, but our entire team versus the government. That can make a difference.

When the lawyer knows someone has their back and the client knows their lawyer has their back, everyone goes into court confident, strategic, on a mission to win. I like to think that our clients aren't just hiring one attorney, they're getting the team. For example, we recently had one of our team staff meetings, and there were five of us, including three former prosecutors and one attorney with five years as a Philadelphia defense attorney, analyzing upcoming cases, going back and forth on strategies and options to help our clients -- not many people do that.

On every case that comes to our office; whether I meet with the client or not, the attorneys prepare an opening confidential memo that is distributed to me and the other attorneys in order to review the case and determine potential issues, defenses and options. Regardless of the seriousness of the case, our goal is to give the client the benefit of our team. Through the use of technology, we can accommodate and keep an eye on properly handling our defense and advocacy on those cases.

DEFINITION OF A DUI IN PENNSYLVANIA

A lay person definition of a DUI is when someone is in control of the operation of a motor vehicle while they're inebriated to a degree that makes them incapable of driving safely, or they have a blood-alcohol level that's above a legal limit. If an officer thinks you look intoxicated and you have alcohol in your system and are incapable of driving, he can charge you.

Does an officer need to "Mirandize" you? From watching TV shows, we always think about Miranda rights, which is the right to remain silent. A common question that clients will ask us is if the cop, the police officer, or the trooper violated my rights because he was asking me all these questions and never Mirandized me.

DUI is unique because it is, in many cases, an observational crime in which the observer is the enforcer of the violation, the police officer. It's a situation in which the officer is in a position to be both advocate and authority; by advocate, I mean his description of what happened can help result in a guilty plea, which means what the officer says should be carefully scrutinized. An officer hasn't met you before, doesn't know how long you were up that night, doesn't know if you were in a smoky room and that's why your eyes are bloodshot, doesn't know if you are generally excitable, and doesn't know whether or not you have a disability that might cause you to walk in a way he considers abnormal.

There's no guarantee the officer will even write it down in his report if you tell them you were up all night, or you have a broken ankle, or problems with your knees. The impetus all of a sudden, though those potential defenses are there, is to feel the weight of the government because now, despite the fact that you're innocent until proven guilty, the assumption in the eyes of the regular Joe is that you are guilty.

Based on the sheer number of DUI cases we take, it's difficult to say whether most DUI's are high BAC versus low BAC; we basically get a variety. However, we've had many cases in which the BAC is 0.081 or 0.085, with the legal limit being 0.08. I'm not aware of any situations in which the result was so close to the limit that the police let them go or just drove them home. In my experience, it's a red line. If you're 0.080 or higher, you'll be arrested

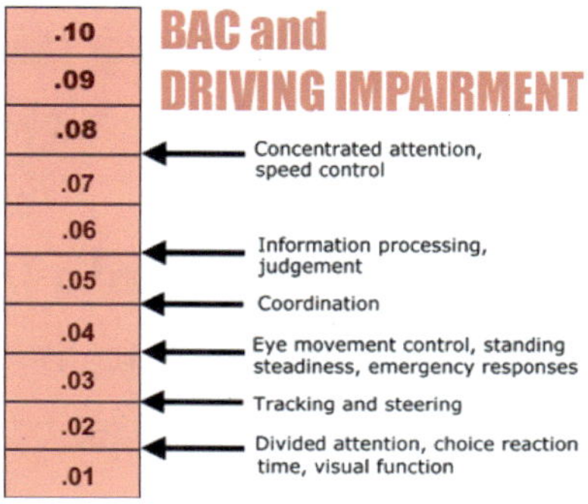

The Highest BAC Level In A DUI Case

One factor that must be acknowledged is that we live in a world in which people have dependency issues that include both controlled substances and alcohol. There are alcoholics who are going through some very difficult times and I've dealt with some high BAC levels that are very high, above 0.30 above 0.40, and those difficult situations often call for a rehabilitative approach rather than a strict defensive approach because the impact of the alcohol or the substances is so obvious that the strength of the advocate is in getting the person treatment versus trying to argue that they weren't intoxicated.

To give you an example of a very interesting trial I had, I can go back in time to my first trial 25 years ago, which involved someone with a BAC of 0.27, which is very high. Back then, the BAC limit was 0.10, and back then, Pennsylvania calibrated a DUI record on a 10-year basis, which means that a first offense DUI has a lesser penalty than a second or third offense DUI within a ten-year period. Currently, if you have a BAC that's twice the legal limit, 0.16, and you accumulate a total of three DUIs within a ten-year period, you're looking at a minimum of 12 months in a state correctional facility -- it's very much been criminalized.

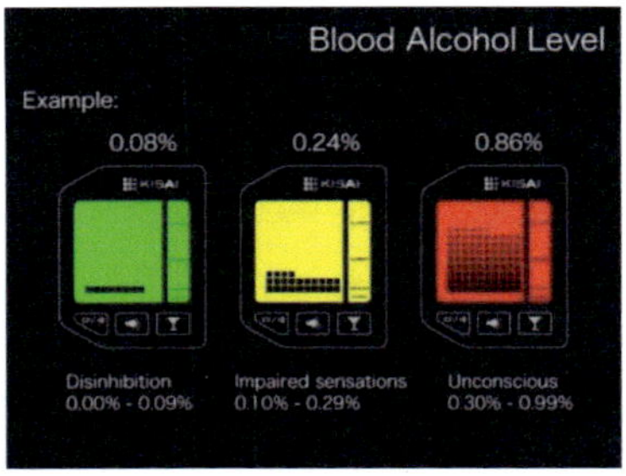

However, 25 years ago the law said that if you got four DUIs over seven years, you faced state jail time. I was dealing with a gentleman who was facing his fourth DUI within seven years, so we're talking about a lot of DUIs, and he was found passed out by himself in a car that was involved in an accident on an abandoned highway at two o'clock in the morning. They wanted to give him state jail time and it didn't look like a good case, but I investigated and found some things that were odd about the case.

For example, he wasn't in the driver's seat; it was one of those cars that basically had a row seat in the front and he was in the middle. As I started learning more, I determined that there had been another driver, who had fled. During the jury trial, when the officer took great pains to argue that this guy's blood alcohol level was 0.27, I actually amped it up as I cross examined him, leading the officer to surmise that with a blood alcohol that high he could or should have been unconscious. You could even argue he was too intoxicated to drive, and the officer bit on it and acknowledged there was no way he could have driven because his blood alcohol level was so high. After establishing that my client was too intoxicated to drive, I introduced a witness, who testified that in fact he was the driver, but fled. This case appears to be an example of a rush to judgement, where the officer assumed our client was the driver without properly investigating the case. The result was an acquittal.

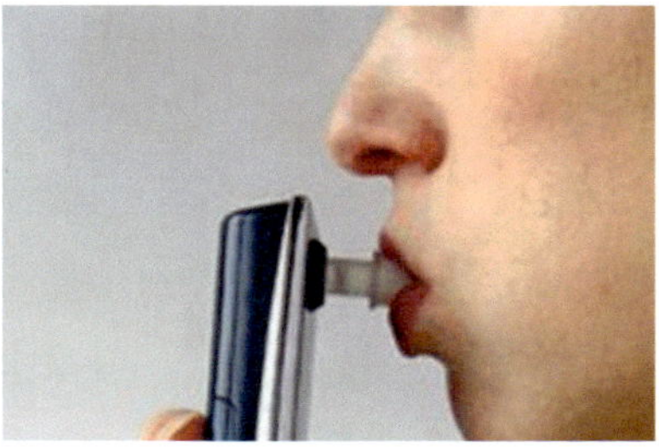

Every case is unique and every case is personal. If the lawyer is not principled, passionate, open minded and hardworking, he or she won't get the best results. The key is to try your best constantly; that's what we do at our office.

Stereotypical DUI Defendant In Pennsylvania

A DUI is unique, in that many people don't want to think of it as a crime. For example, Chester County is the most affluent county in Pennsylvania, but wealth is not a probibitive factor in the context of DUIs. Our area has a very high DUI rate and the people who get DUIs are typically first time offenders, people in their 30s, 40s or 50s, who get caught in the wrong place at the wrong time. This is because we live in a world in which you go to a restaurant and have 2 glasses of wine with dinner and now all of a sudden you're driving home and you're a danger or at risk of a DUI!

Most of my clients are not a 0.27 BAC, but in that lower to mid-range who are coming home from dinner or party, who otherwise would not be driving inebriated, or who didn't think they were over the level; the bar or restaurant certainly didn't think they were over the level because in Pennsylvania law, bartenders and waiters and waitresses are prohibited from serving anyone who appears intoxicated. Despite this, they get pulled over and told that they're over the legal limit. That is a good part of our practice.

Another developing area of our practice is people who are on prescription medication and are pulled over. In Pennsylvania, the fact that a drug is a prescription medication does not exempt you from getting a DUI. There's been an increase in those types of DUIs in my practice area in the greater Philadelphia area. The most common thing I hear with prescription medication DUIs is that the person told the judge or the officer that they weren't drinking, but taking medicine, believing that the fact that the medicine is a prescription is a defense, without realizing that they're basically admitting they're under the influence of an intoxicant.

With regard to restaurants and bars, in Pennsylvania there's a law called the dram shop law, which makes a bar or restaurant responsible if they serve someone who is visibly intoxicated and that person gets involved in an accident. Our personal injury department actually takes those types of cases, prosecuting the money makers for over-serving clients, though clearly they have an obligation to the public and to their patrons not to serve them too much alcohol.

THE TOP MISCONCEPTIONS ABOUT BEING ARRESTED FOR DUI

Not everyone realizes that a DUI is actually a crime, a misdemeanor offense. In the event of a conviction of a misdemeanor, it is not subject to expungement. In Pennsylvania and most other states, there is an Internet-based court docketing service which allows you to quickly search and determine if someone has a criminal record. This means that, if someone has been charged with a DUI, it will likely show up immediately on this public docketing service and it will stay there until the charges are dismissed and expunged. In the event of a conviction, it will remain on your record until such time that you successfully petition for a pardon from the governor. The pardon process can take three to four years.

A DUI has the impact of a scarlet letter. It may be an unspoken factor employers use in deciding on hiring or retaining your services. Could an employer use your DUI record in considering if you are someone they can count on, who will show up for work every day and who can drive. That conviction may prevent you from even getting an interview and you'll never know why, because the conviction record is so readily available that an employer can look at it and just exclude that person. That's one thing people don't anticipate with a DUI, and they don't realize that, being a crime, there is mandatory jail time. They hear about first time offender programs, but not everyone is eligible for one; they believe it refers to their first DUI, but it refers to their first time involvement with the court system.

In Chester County for example, if you have any prior misdemeanor or felony convictions within 10 years of the date of a DUI, you're ineligible for the first time offender program. It could be a big deal if you were a

college kid and charged with possession of a small amount of marijuana, you admitted guilt and paid a small fine and 8 years later you get a DUI. You're thinking to yourself, 8 years is a lifetime, but to the court it's not. You'll be facing, at minimum a weekend in jail, loss of your license for a year and a criminal record forever. In a tough job market, that's the straw that breaks the camel's back, and what prevents you from getting that top job. In this age of no privacy, any involvement with the law puts an individual at risk, as far as opportunities go, which is why we have to take a DUI very seriously; we can't even anticipate how it will be viewed ten years from now.

The first mistake you can make after getting charged with a DUI is not taking it seriously or trying to ignore or deny how a DUI can impact you. The first thing you should do is speak to an experienced DUI lawyer, or better yet, a DUI legal team, who can answer your questions, and explain to you your rights, your options and the benefits of their representation.

Human Insight Gained From Handling DUI Cases

The best way to explain it is -- it's a surreal experience for most people; being pulled over, being asked questions and being led by the police officer. They feel lost. They can't believe it's all happening. Then, they're taken to the hospital for a blood test. Next they're finger-printed and being live-scanned. These are all things they just can't imagine are happening when they happen.

Even the next day when they wake up, they're like, did this really happen? That is the most common experience clients have, in part because most people think of themselves as good people, and good people don't get arrested by the police. It's hard for someone getting arrested, especially for a DUI, to believe they just committed a crime.

Remember, you are not a criminal but you are accused of a serious criminal offense and you need the benefit of an attorney, or better yet, a legal team, passionate about your case, compassionate about your circumstances, and ready to fight for your rights.

Public Knowledge Of DUI Charges

As a practical matter an arrest is a public event; all courts in the US are public if a matter involves someone over 18. You can walk in to any court at any time, civil or criminal, unless there's a very specific reason preventing it, and you can discuss what you see. Newspapers need to fill pages, and one easy way to do so is with a police blotter, naming those who have been charged with offenses.

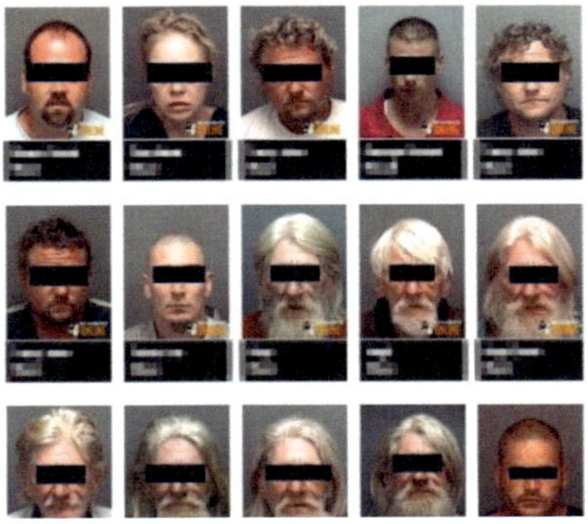

Twenty years ago, if you lived in Philadelphia and you were travelling to Lancaster and got a DUI, it would be in the Lancaster news and nobody would know about it. Today, it goes online, which means, regardless of where you get the DUI, your name will pop up and those who see it will know you've been arrested for these offenses. There will be a public record of your arrest and you face the prospect of being prejudiced by that public record.

You need a team of attorneys that are experienced and aggressive in fighting for your rights, contesting the police arrest and charges, and working to avoid a criminal conviction so that you have the right to get that public record removed.

Common Mistakes Committed After A DUI Arrest

Everyone should be a very careful driver, which means a significant reduction in the likelihood of being pulled over. A common story I hear is that someone swerved because they dropped their phone, or were lighting a cigarette, or turning on the radio. Those types of distractions aren't necessarily related to drinking, but they gave the officer a reason to pull them over, and honestly, if it's after 9 o'clock at night or very early morning, the officer will have a heightened expectation that a driver who fails to drive appropriately is doing so because they're under the influence of some kind of intoxicant.

The same distractions during the day won't necessarily result in being pulled over by an officer because they'll figure it's just someone who's not paying attention, but at 2 a.m. -- drunk driver. The best thing someone can do is to be extra careful when driving, which seems simple enough; if the officer has no reason to stop you, there's no DUI. This is common sense, and a good gauge of your ability to drive before you get in the car, which is critical.

In Pennsylvania, the use of marijuana is illegal. That much you should already know. But many people do not realize that it is illegal to smoke marijuana and then drive. In fact, a DUI can result from the ingestion of

either prescription and/or illegal controlled substances. In the event that a police officer has reason to believe that you are under the influence of a controlled substance, he will request a drug scan.

Many individuals facing a marijuana related DUI are doing so because they made the mistake of keeping marijuana and/or marijuana paraphernalia in their car. Don't be foolish enough to carry marijuana in your motor vehicle, so that if you're pulled over, the officer can smell it and have grounds to arrest you for driving after imbibing marijuana. To be charged with a DUI for marijuana, the interesting thing in Pennsylvania is, you don't have to be smoking while driving.

In Pennsylvania, it's not like some old Cheech and Chong movie where the car's all filled with smoke while they're being pulled over; they may have smoked a marijuana cigarette two days earlier, and just have the THC in their system, but they end up getting convicted of a DUI because of that.

If you are facing a marijuna-related DUI, speak to an attorney immediately to discuss your rights, which could include the legality of a search and the use of evidence against you. You need a team of attorneys that are experienced and aggressive in fighting for your rights, and contesting the police arrest, search and charges.

Step-By-Step Breakdown Of DUI Process In Pennsylvania

First, an officer has to be able to articulate a violation of the traffic code to substantiate pulling someone over; they can't simply pull someone over because they look suspicious; there has to be something they can explain as a violation of law. Once they pull that person over,

they're allowed to ask for their ID and insurance and they can take a flash light and look into to the car. At that point, the officer is looking to use their senses to see if they smell alcohol, or some kind of intoxicant like marijuana.

When the person speaks, police will likely interpret any slurring, and/or dilation of pupils, as a sign of intoxication. If police determine that the person is showing signs of intoxication, they will request that they exit their vehicle and perform one or several types of sobriety tests to assess their coordination and thought process.

It is not clear that Pennsylvania law or your privilege to drive requires you to submit to field sobriety tests. A sobriety test is different than a blood test, in that implied consent places an obligation on you submitting to a chemical test. Is there really a benefit to performing a sobriety test, where the tests being conducted are a very subjective analysis by an officer who is pursuing a DUI.

When an officer believes he has sufficient evidence to arrest someone for a DUI, he will request a chemical test such as a breath or blood test. In Pennsylvania, you imlicitly consent to a DUI in exchange for your privilege to drive a motor vehicle. To keep that privilege you must abide by the Department of Transportation's standard, which means you implicitly consent to submit to a chemcial test if a police officer has sufficient evidence to believe you are intoxicated.

Regardless of whether you believe the police officer has rightfully arrested you, if an officer asks for a blood or breathalyzer test, it's almost always the best policy to submit to it. In Pennsylvania, if you refuse to submit to a blood or breathalyzer test and a court of law determines that it was properly requested, you will likely lose your license for 12 months over and above any penalty for the

DUI. In addition, if you refuse to submit to a blood test, the government can use that refusal against you in its prosecution of you for a DUI and the refusal can also impact the penalty you face.

Pennsylvania has different levels of DUI; including general impairment for Driving While Intoxicated (DWI) to a level that renders you Incapable of Safe Driving, with a blood-alcohol level of 0.08-0.10, which is what we typically call low, whereas a blood-alcohol level between 0.10 and 0.15 is considered high and a blood-alcohol level of 0.16 or higher is the highest. You will also be charged at the highest level if there's a controlled substance in your system, you refused a test, you're a commercial driver, or you're under 21 years.

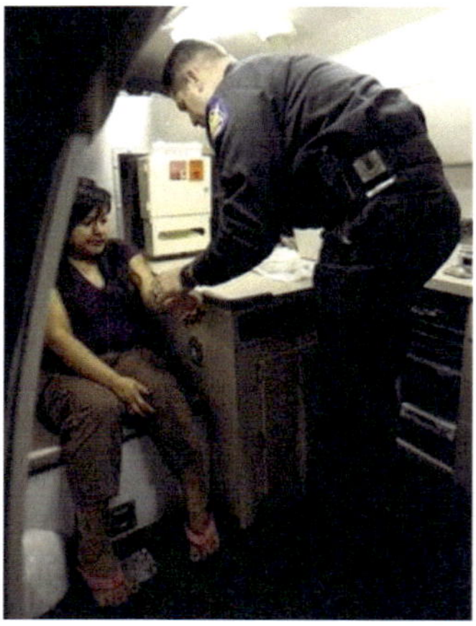

If an officer wants a blood test, the best option is almost always to submit to the test and have your lawyer contest the legality of the arrest or the stop, or contest the legality of the request for a blood test.

Standardized Field Sobriety Tests In Pennsylvania

Standardized field sobriety tests are endorsed by the National Highway Traffic and Safety Administration; the typical tests that are considered are the horizontal gaze nystagmus, often known as the HGN test, the walk and turn test and the one leg stand test. Generally speaking, in this part of a DUI prosecution, the police officer testifies that he is an expert, even though the testimony is often self-serving.

Generally the judge will accept his testimony as expert because, in Pennsylvania law, the standard for an expert is very loose. It's ultimately up to a judge or jury, a fact finder, to consider the weight of the expert's testimony.

At a jury trial, the judge will let the jury decide whether he is an expert; the problem is, the typical prejudice is that the jury is hearing from the officer who's dressed in his fine blues, and he is claiming that he's unbiased and is just telling it the way it is -- this guy was drunk.

It makes a DUI different from many criminal cases; it's the officer versus you, and there may not be another witness, which is why it's easy to get a little cynical -- you have the government making so much money from DUIs in which the only witness is a government witness.

The Impact Of A Police Witness In A DUI Trial

It will always have a big impact on a jury. That's why, before a case goes to trial there is a preliminary hearing in which the police and the government have to establish prima facie evidence to support the case, meaning they have to show that they have established the elements of a crime. A preliminary hearing is something of a gate keeper process to prevent someone from going to trial when the government, by their own admission, lacks sufficient evidence to move forward.

For example, we had a case a few weeks ago in which the police came to the scene of a car accident and there were two individuals there, and both looked intoxicated. However, the officer never asked either one if they were the driver; the officer assumed the man was the driver and never even took a blood test results from the woman.

At the preliminary hearing, through tough cross examination by our office, the officer admitted he could not say with specificity that our client had actually operated the motor vehicle, and in fact, it could possibly have been the other person since he had no way to prove who was driving. The magistrate dismissed the case.

Individuals facing a DUI in the greater Philadelphia metro area could actually be subject to two different court systems; the Philadelphia Court System, and the Pennsylvania Court System for suburban Philadelphia and the rest of the state. In Philadelphia, if someone is arrested for a DUI, it is likely that you will be held in custody for a 24-hour period in a detention facility nicknamed the "round house", where you will wait until you are arraigned and released on bail. Someone who has been accused, but not yet been found guilty, is incarcerated for up to 24 hours waiting for bail, then they're released, and the charges are set.

In the rest of the state, once the police obtain either your breath test which is through an intoxilyzer device at the police station, or you're taken to the hospital for a blood or urine test, you will often be processed and then released pending the filing and scheduling of a preliminary hearing. Processsing usually includes being finger printed, often on a device called a live scan, which actually electronically scans them into a federal database, and your picture is taken. If someone's there to take you home, you'll be released; otherwise you have to wait in custody until someone comes to get you or the police determine you're no longer intoxicated.

Many people are surprised that they are not given a ticket or other paperwork after their arrest.

In Pennsylvania, a misdemeanor DUI is normally served by regular and certified mail, along with a notice to appear in court, called a summons, for the preliminary hearing. Once you receive the summons, very commonly your hearing will be scheduled about 2 months after your arrest, mainly because there is currently a 6-8 week wait for the police to get the results of the blood test.

The long wait for the results is something that is very confusing for most clients. They're familiar with going to the hospital for a blood test and getting the results immediately. However, in the context of a criminal prosecution, the government is seeking to create a chain of custody to establish that the blood results belong to the accused. They attempt to do this by placing the blood into a forensic kit, taped and sending it to a forensic lab. Furthermore, it's done in a way that the government can say that there is chain of custody, that the blood definitely came from you and not from someone else. For budget reasons, there are currently only a few forensic labs that do this, so it can take weeks to get the results back.

The preliminary hearing is an event for which an individual does have to show, and they should definitely show with an attorney. It's an opportunity to either contest the charges and the elements of the charges, or it's an opportunity for the lawyer to talk to the district attorney about eligibility for programs

that avoid conviction, such as the accelerated rehabilitative disposition program or ARD. ARD is a nontribal disposition program that does not require an accused to admit guilty or accept quilty and allows them an opportunity to get the charges to be dismissed and be eligible for expungement after a period of probation and conditions.

Often, a candidate for a DUI related ARD must agree to give up their license for a short period of time in exchange for the charges to ultimately be dropped.

Discussion of eligibility for ARD can happen at a preliminary hearing, but one thing that will absolutely happen is that someone will be placed on bail. Even for a misdemeanor DUI, there is a requirement under the Pennsylvania criminal code that an accused be placed on bail. There are different types of bail: there's the cash bail, there's 10% bail, which means you put up 10% of the bail amount. The most unrestrictive type of bail is ROR bail (Released on your Own Recognizance). Many of our DUI clients facing their first contact with the law are afforded, ROR bail.

An ROR bail is common for our clients when the judge sees the client as a first time offender, who is represented by able counsel who will keep the client and the court notified of all developments; thus creating a low concern that the client will not show up.

ROR bail is a more favorable option for someone who retains counsel right away, appears at all necessary hearings, and doesn't give the court any reason to be concerned that the person will flee. Once the preliminary hearing is complete, the case is transfered from the local magistrate level to the county court house. In Philadelphia, the case will transfer to the criminal justice center.

The DMV And Ignition Interlock Device In Pennsylvania

One of the most significant non-criminal penalties a DUI can bring is the impact it will have on the driver's license. In Pennsylvania, if you are facing a first offense of DUI and you are convicted of a DUI and your blood alcohol is 0.10 or higher, you face a mandatory license suspension of one year. This means you cannot drive a motor vehicle under any circumstances during that time, with no exceptions -- not an emergency, to get to work, nothing. If you're caught driving a motor vehicle during this time frame, you will face a 60-90 day jail sentence and an additional 12 month license suspension.

It doesn't stop there. Over the past few years the penalties have actually increased, which means it is a common experience that, when you get your license back, you have to install an ignition interlock system for another 12 months. This device requires you to blow into it in order to start the car, and if there is a positive reading the car will not start. You also have to blow into it at random times while you're driving or the car will start beeping, the horn will go on, the lights will start flashing and you'll be giving police an opportunity to pull you over.

If you blow into it and you're positive, the same will happen and if you are caught driving without an ignition interlock, or you try to circumvent the ignition interlock system there are more charges possible. In Chester County, even if you're a first time offender, if your blood-alcohol level was high, like a 0.30, there is a new provision that says you must install an ignition interlock as a condition for entry into the ARD program.

It probably goes without saying that ignition interlock is not free. Assuming you can find a company that will lease it to you; you may be looking at costs in excess of $1200 to $1500. There is also the concern of whether the ignition interlock will impact your motor vehicle insurance. You have to worry whether your insurance rates will go up if they know you have an ignition interlock and a DUI.

ARE THERE ANY LAWS THAT ADDRESS A DRIVER WITH A BAC BELOW 0.08 IN PENNSYLVANIA?

The original DUI statute says that, if you're operating a motor vehicle and you are incapable of driving safely due to intoxication, you're guilty of a DUI; that is section 3802 (a) and it's the first part of the DUI statute.

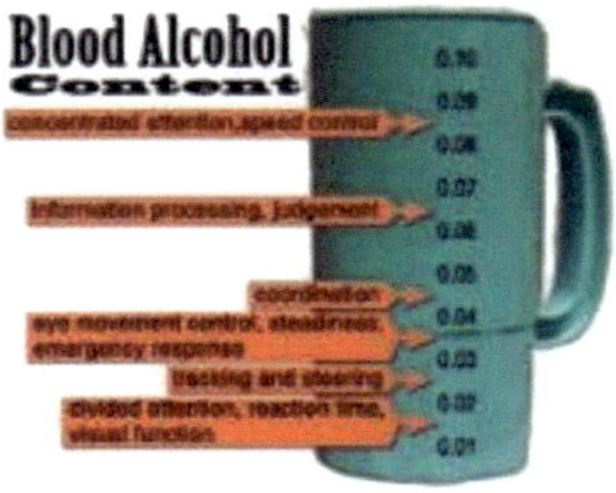

There's no mention of blood-alcohol level. An officer's "expert opinion" of safe driving is necessary to support his belief that you're drinking and that you're unable to hold your liquor. Someone can have a blood alcohol level under 0.08 and still get a DUI in Pennsylvania. There is a provision in the statute that says if your blood alcohol level is 0.05 or higher and you appear intoxicated, you can still get a DUI, so if someone is at 0.05, but an officer testifies that they look intoxicated and they're incapable of safe driving, you may face a DUI.

The cases we're most concerned about are those in which there is a motor vehicle accident, or when there is clear evidence of someone's erratic driving preceding their arrest. Pennsylvania allows for sobriety check points, and if you approach one and either stop or are pulled over and the police have reason to believe you're intoxicated and your breath test results were 0.05, they'll have difficulty establishing that you were incapable of safe driving because they didn't witness you driving unsafely.

The cases in which someone's involved in an accident where the officer can point to the accident to show that, with a blood alcohol level of 0.05, it's his opinion that alcohol caused the accident and that's a tough case to win because no one is sympathetic. People can be sympathetic about someone getting a DUI at a sobriety check point who has a 0.09, they can be sympathetic about someone who's on medication and was unaware that it is illegal to operate a motor vehicle after they have ingested a prescription narcotic. It is not a defense, but the jury may be sympathetic. However, when someone gets hurt or injured, you've lost the jury.

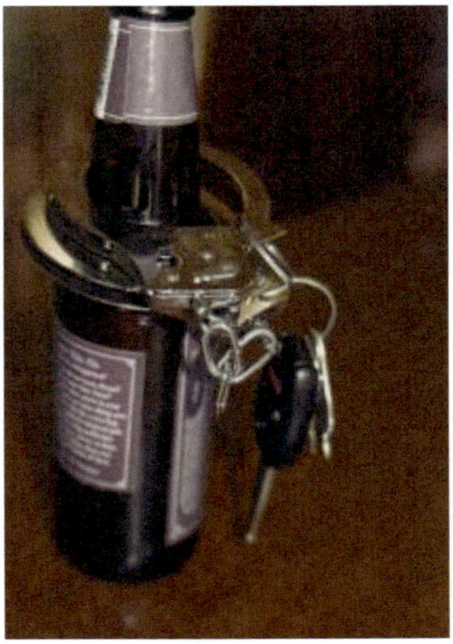

THE POTENTIAL PENALTIES ASSOCIATED WITH DUI CHARGES IN PENNSYLVANIA

If you're looking at a first offense DUI, what we want to do first is to break down between the lowest tier, which is under 0.10, with no minimum jail time, and the maximum possible

period of incarceration or supervision, which on a first offense DUI is six months. There is no mandatory minimum jail time for someone with a blood alcohol level under 0.10, and there is no license suspension. For someone with a blood alcohol level of 0.10 to 0.159 it is still a six month period of supervision, but the mandatory minimum sentence is 48 hours in jail and there's a 12 month license suspension with a conviction.

With a highest tier DUI, the mandatory minimum increases to 72 hours and there is still a 12 month license suspension. In Pennsylvania, if you get a second DUI within 10 years from the date you are convicted or placed on ARD for the first, all penalties increase in dramatic fashion to between five days and 90 days in jail, and if you get a third DUI within that ten year period, the jail time increases to a mandatory minimum of 10 days to 12 months, and those are the minimums.

Aggravating And Mitigating Factors For DUI Charges

Over time, there have been more DUI charges added, such as a DUI aggravated assault, which means, if you are DUI and you cause serious injuries to someone, you can be charged with a felony

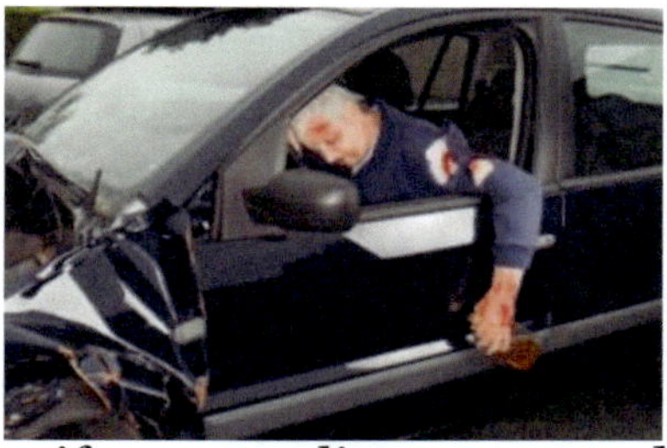

level aggravated assault DUI, or if your negligence caused someone's death, you'll face vehicular homicide DUI with the first offense being three years in state jail.

These aggravated factors will likely result in more serious charges. Other examples of aggravating events include if a driver is intoxicated and has young kids in the car. Regardless of whether there's an accident, it's considered reckless endangerment of children. Even someone with no criminal history will be ineligible for a probationary program like ARD.

DIVERSIONARY PROGRAMS AVAILABLE FOR FIRST TIME DUI OFFENDERS

Every county in Pennsylvania has some authority to create diversionary programs, so first and foremost, it's important to note the difference between ARD and these other programs. ARD is a means to avoid a conviction, whereas the other programs are means to reduce the impact of the punishment. We can fight a case by getting it thrown out on a legal basis or at trial, or we can get someone on the ARD program. If we can argue, for example, that the officer didn't have a legal basis and the stop was illegal, we can throw the case out on legal grounds, or we can go to trial and convince the jury that the prosecution hasn't proven their case, or we can apply for ARD. The other programs tend to involve a conviction.

There are also circumstances where we can avoid a conviction whether an individual has a drug dependency and we are able to gain entry into the ARD program as long as they also agree to partipate in Drug Court or a related program. Drug Court is a secondary program that will last at least 12 months and which requires the active participation of an individual to show up at least once a week and do regular urine tests to basically take active steps to change their patterns and avoid drug use.

A program that we use very commonly in a case, in which we are looking for some kind of negotiated deal, is a program called the intermediate punishment program (IPP), which is a means of redefining incarceration. We've already talked briefly about what the seriousness of the mandatory minimum penalties is, with a second offense DUI bringing up to 90 days in confinement and a third offense bringing a minimum twelve month confinement.

Intermediate punishment enables a judge to redefine confinement as home monitoring. This means a judge, instead of giving someone 90 days in jail, may put them in jail for a reduced period of time, with the rest of the time staying at home and wearing a home monitoring device.

The ARD or First Time Offender Program In Pennsylvania

The ARD program, or the first time offender program, is for someone with no criminal history, to avoid a trial or admission of guilt. The program can last anywhere from 6-12 months (or longer) and all someone in ARD has to do is effectively stay out of trouble for a period of time, agree to certain voluntary penalties and at the end of the probationary period the charges will be dropped.

For a client who is 35, has no criminal record and was pulled over with a blood alcohol level of 0.18, he will face 72 hours in jail, a permanent criminal record, a loss of license for 12 months, and an impact on his insurance, but instead, he can come to us and we can negotiate his entry into the ARD program. He agrees to an alcohol evaluation, to safe driving classes, he agrees to pay a fine of about $1,500, which is about how much he would pay if convicted, he agrees to voluntarily surrender his license for two months rather than 12, and he agrees to stay out of trouble for six months, which is something he has done his entire life. At the end of the six months the charges are dismissed, he is eligible to get those charges expunged and he can move on with his life.

As part of our initial meeting and case assessment with a client, we try to establish whether the case is defendable -- can we attack the legality of the stop or the arrest, the legality of the blood test and the merits of the defense versus the penalty. We take the time to reflect on whether this is a good case to bring to trial, and then we can bring that information to our client so they can make the best decision for themselves. In every case, whether it's a first offense DUI or its fourth offense DUI, we want to give the client reliable advice, counsel and leadership.

It's the client's case, but they are looking for someone to lead and give them advice. They are not looking for someone to simply tell them what the law is. They are looking for someone to give them direction and that's what we do every single day with every case we have.

Once a program like ARD is off the table, trial is always a worthy option, and in my experience and the experience of my team, it is rare that a judge will penalize you for asserting your right to trial. DUI's are very different from many other offenses. Drug possession charges have no mandatory minimum in Pennsylvania. You can assault someone and there's no mandatory minimum, but a DUI has mandatory minimums, so in many cases, when we have a client facing a mandatory 90 days or more in jail, it behooves them to find experienced counsel to contest the charges and be prepared to go to trial.

People like to think that, if police have a case, they should win. That's not the same thing as the government proving their case, and making their case in front of a jury. A good advocate always puts the pressure back on the government. We can't just assume they're going to win, and a client facing mandatory jail time can't just say, well, if the police, if the district attorney does everything they're supposed to do, they'll probably lose; that's what a trial is for. It's to place the burden back where it belongs -- on the prosecution, which is where an individual gets his or her leverage, by making the government prove its case.

I've had numerous jury trials in which I walked in with doubt, but there's a certitude that we have to fight this, and once we were in the middle of the trial, a weakness in the prosecution's case was exposed, and we capitalized on it. It's a good thing to go to trial; if we can say with a degree of certitude based on our experience that the judge won't penalize you for asserting your right to trial, then the choice between a mandatory penalty or going to trial makes trial an excellent option.

In a time where we always have to worry about the government abusing its power, going to trial is a way to keep the government honest, of putting police officers in their places if they try to become advocates rather than officers of the law.

Advice For People Contemplating A Guilty Plea In A DUI

Many individuals want to move on, and it's our job to explain the implications of their actions, so they can make an intelligent decision that's in the best interests of themselves and their families. If we look at some of the things we've discussed, anyone facing a DUI needs to consider the implications of the conviction on their record, the impact on their driver's license, the loss of privileges, the impact of possibly going to jail on their family, the humiliation and the impact not only of this offense but on some possible future offense which will have much more severe penalties.

In the past, I had a client who was almost cavalier, saying he didn't want to fight; he just wanted to get this done, because they had a good case. It's important for me to talk to them about fighting their case so they're not in a situation eight years from now in which they get a second offense DUI that wouldn't be a second offense DUI if they had fought the first one. Ultimately, my client's the boss, but we want our boss to be informed, to make good decisions, and it's our role to basically help them make decisions that benefit themselves and their family.

PREPARING A DEFENDANT FOR A DUI TRIAL

When someone calls or emails our office, or office strives to respond immediately, learn about their needs and schedule a free initial consultation. We live in a society trained to look for the "best price" and it is

common for some people to call looking for "prices". I am a believer in providing a free initial consultation that includes meeting with our prospective client, discussing the facts, how the government will likely prosecute the case, the penalties he like faces, and the strategies that we can take on his behalf. It is during this time that a prospective client can best learn whether we are the best advocates for his defense and also confirm that our services are within his budget. We try to avoid talking about prices first; we want to talk about the substance of the DUI first to get a sense that the client understands what they face. We talk about how we can help, which is why we suggest that they come in and meet with us for a consultation, which is an opportunity to sit down with them and sometimes their family, talk about the specifics of the case, and talk more about their background -- things that you can't get from an email or phone call.

People are sometimes uncomfortable talking about issues over the phone or in email, and we need to clearly define whether or not they have a prior criminal record and, if so, what impact it will have on these new charges. We also want to discuss potential issues that could arise and, once they engage us, we draft a comprehensive and confidential memorandum so that all of the other attorneys can start reviewing and discussing it and talk about this person's options. As the case progresses, we discuss the case and talk about things that can be done. Sometimes it will be about getting an expert, like a blood test expert or a toxicologist; in some cases, it may be an accident reconstruction expert.

In some cases, we may want to hire an investigator to look at witnesses and examine the actual facts of the case. In some cases, we may have to hire a psychologist or get a narrative report from a medical provider who can assist us. Working collectively as a team, we can discuss all options from our different perspectives so that we're putting our client into the best possible scenario.

How Often Can You Get DUI Charges Dropped, Dismissed or Reduced?

It is our goal to get charges reduced or dismissed and I am very proud of our ability to get charges and/or punishment regularly reduced or dismissed. When people talk to me, they'll ask me how successful we are, and the

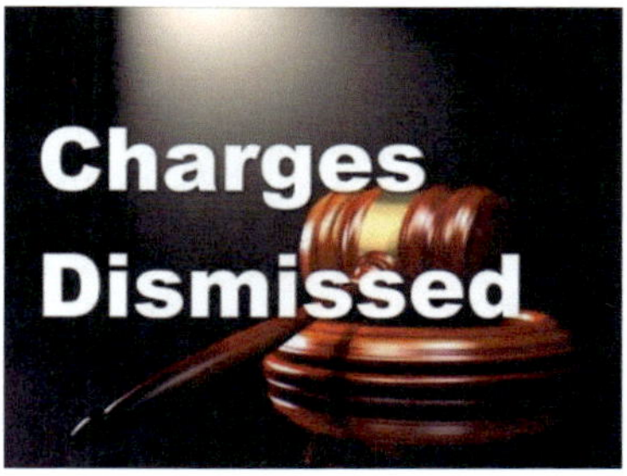

honest answer is, every case is individual and a victory is different for every single case. In some cases, victory is defined by the charges being dismissed, while in other cases victory is defined by avoiding a license suspension or conviction and in some cases it means getting the felony charge dropped when someone faces one on top of a DUI.

Hiring An Experienced Private Attorney Or Retaining A Public Defender?

One issue that everyone has to deal with is an economic one. No one saves up for a lawyer, and no one has a special bag of money for when they make a mistake, so one difficulty people have is budgeting for a lawyer. As far as handling a case themselves, while we live in an Internet world, where you can look up everything, a web page is not a lawyer, and information is not wisdom.

Likewise, are you that confident that what you see on websites will give you the judgment and wisdom to basically be your own advocate? You need someone on your side, or better yet a team. It isn't simply about knowing the law; it's about having an experienced advocate who has your back and has what it takes to fight on your behalf. You need someone who cares about you, but who is also objective and who can act on your behalf. Everyone needs this when going into court.

There are many great public defenders, but the main concern people have about a public defender is that they're so overwhelmed by cases or a lack of organization that they can't focus on your case, and they can't be available when you reach out to them. It's more of a systematic problem with solo practitioners and public defenders, not an indictment on those individuals who are in those roles.

Ultimately, the government has a team of lawyers working toward the goal of convicting you and you should have a team of lawyers working on your behalf, protecting your rights and serving to gain you justice.

Case Studies Of DUI Cases Handled In Pennsylvania

Our team has handled thousands of DUI cases and we are proud of our record and our devotion to serve them well. Our team has won cases at trial, in suppression motions and at the preliminary hearing. We have gotten cases thrown out in which the police officer failed to articulate grounds for the stop; and cases that were thrown out at the preliminary hearing because we made the government try to prove their case. Our firm is built to handle simple and complex cases.

I could probably spend hours talking about different victories we've had; victories for our clients, in which we gave them a second opportunity and that's as important as anything. The secret for me and my team is that we do care, and we are grateful when our clients are grateful. That motivates us to do well -- it's the ultimate motivation for us. If you're motivated by doing good and you're motivated by helping people, the business end takes care of itself. So, yes, we are a successful practice, because our priorities are with our clients.

What Makes Your Firm Unique In Handling DUI Cases?

If I was looking for an attorney, I would want to make sure that the attorney was experienced in DUI Law and was well respected by the clients that retained him. I would want to look for a DUI attorney with a significant number of positive reviews, not just from other lawyers who are patting their friends on the back and saying he's a good guy, but reviews based on client feedback. Starting with a very simplistic or common sense approach is a good start. If you read up on the lawyers, do they go to court every day and fight DUIs? Is it a general practice lawyer or someone who is a DUI defense specialist, and do they have specific experience like our team, who are former prosecutors who now defend DUI cases. Also, are you best served by hiring a solo practioner who may be overwhelmed by his schedule vs a team of lawyers working in concert on your behalf and as an effective balance to the government's team of prosecutors?

There's value in having the right type of former prosecutor as part of your team. Being a former prosecutor isn't the end all. In fact, there are many former prosecutors who go into private practice and become DUI players, the kind who know you're guilty, because they used to prosecute such people, but they promise to walk you to your sentencing, and you don't want that. You want someone with a fight in their heart, who is a bit of an idealist, who is sympathetic and compassionate and enjoys fighting for justice. You want someone willing to fight, not just the facts of your case, but also the punishment.

We need for the judge or jury to understand that you're a real person, not that photo the police took on your worst day but a good person, worthy of redemption, and you shouldn't be subjected to the worst punishment. That's part of what an advocate is, so if you can have a team of advocates who care about you and about what happens, who have a desire to succeed not just for themselves but for their clients, then you're taking the right steps and making the right decision about hiring a DUI defense attorney.

DISCLAIMER

This publication is intended to be informational only. No legal advice is being given, and no attorney-client relationship is intended to be created by reading this material. If you are facing legal issues, whether criminal or civil, seek professional legal counsel to get your questions answered.

Ciccarelli Law Offices
304 North High Street
West Chester, PA 19380
(610) 692-8700
www.ciccarelli.com

Made in the USA
Monee, IL
05 November 2026

67385071R00038